The Ring Bear

by
N. L. Sharp

illustrated by
Timothy James Hantula

D1299835

Published by Prairieland Press
PO Box 2404
Fremont, NE 68026-2404
Printed in the U.S.A.

Original Book Design by Lynn Gibney

ISBN-10: 0-97598291-5
ISBN-13: 978-0-975-98291-4

Prairieland Press™

For Larry, my ring bear prince
and all of our cubs.

—*N. L. Sharp*

Robert *loved* bears. He loved real bears and stuffed bears and bears in books. He loved black bears and brown bears and polar bears. He even loved to eat bears. Graham cracker bears and cinnamon bears and chocolate bears. So he wasn't surprised when his mom said he was going to be the ring bear in his Aunt Jane's wedding.

"What does a ring bear do?" Robert asked.

"You carry the pillow that holds the rings," Mom said.

"What happens if I drop it?" Once, he was carrying his plate to the sink. It dropped, and peas rolled all over the kitchen floor.

"Don't worry," Mom said. "The rings will be tied on tight. Even if you drop the pillow, you won't lose the rings."

"What does a ring bear wear?" Robert asked.

"A suit," Mom said. "A black suit with a tail, a white shirt, and a red bow tie."

Robert smiled. I'll look just like a panda bear, he thought. This was going to be fun!

Robert wanted to be the best ring bear he could, so he practiced every day. He growled at the dog. He ate berries (which were really grapes) and drank honey (which was really apple juice). And he crawled around the house with a pillow on his back, trying to keep his glow-in-the-dark ring from falling on the floor.

Finally, there was only one day left before the wedding.

"Robert, it's time for the rehearsal," Dad said.

"Rehearsal? What's that?"

"The rehearsal is like a play. We're going to practice our parts for the wedding, so tomorrow we'll know just what to do."

"I've been practicing," Robert said. "Every day."

"Good," Dad said. "I'm proud of you. But tonight Aunt Jane wants everyone to practice together."

Robert looked at his clothes. "Where's my suit?" he asked.

"Here it is." Mom took a bag out of the closet. "Try it on, please. We want to make sure that everything fits just right."

Robert stared at himself in the mirror. The black suit did not look like a bear suit to Robert. Instead, it looked like something his dad wore when he went to a fancy party.

"Are you sure this is what I'm supposed to wear?" he asked.

"Yes," Mom said.

"Where's the tail?"

Mom pointed to a long flap on the back of the jacket.

Robert looked at the flap. Then he looked at his bears. Maybe I'm supposed to be a dancing bear, he thought, like in the circus.

"Take it off," Mom said. "We don't want to get it dirty before tomorrow." She hung the suit back in the closet.

Soon it was time to go. Robert wondered where the wedding would be. Would it be in his grandmother's back yard?

Maybe it was in a park or at the zoo!

But the car did not go to any of those places. Instead, his dad drove straight to the church.

"What are we doing here?" Robert asked. "Is this where the wedding will be?"

"Yes," said Mom. "Didn't you know?"

"No!" said Robert. "How can I be a bear when the wedding is in a church?"

"You're not going to be a bear," Mom said. "You're going to be a ring bearer."

"You mean I don't get to wear a bear suit and growl and carry the pillow on my back?"

"No, that would be silly. People don't have bears in their weddings. They have ring bearers."

Robert stomped his foot. ***"No!"*** he said. "I want to be a bear. If I can't be a bear, I'm not going to be in the wedding!"

"You have to be in the wedding," Dad said. "Aunt Jane needs you. She can't get married without those rings."

"Someone else can carry them," Robert said.

"I don't want someone else," Aunt Jane said. "I want you."

Robert sat down on the curb. He thought about how much fun it had been practicing to be a bear. Then he thought about how sad Aunt Jane looked when he said he wasn't going to be in her wedding.

"Is it true you can't get married without those rings?" he asked.

"Yes, Robert, it is," Aunt Jane said.

"And do you really want me to be the one to carry them?"

"Yes, I do. It wouldn't be the same without you."

Robert growled. "All right," he said. "I'll do it."

The next day, Robert wore his black suit with its long tail, white shirt and red bow tie. He carried the pillow down the aisle and held the rings until the minister wanted them. And everyone agreed, he was the **best ring bearer** they had ever seen.

Later, at the reception, he growled at the flower girl.
He ate berries (which were really mints) and drank honey
(which was really
punch). And he
crawled around
with his pillow on
his back, trying to
keep the ring pop
(which his new
Uncle Dan had
given him) from
falling on the
floor.

And everyone agreed, he was the
best ring bear
they had ever seen, too.

Check out Sophie's experience as the flower girl in this wedding!

The Flower Girl

by
N. L. Sharp

illustrated by
Timothy James Hantula

Made in the USA
Middletown, DE
18 April 2022